To: _My sister Harrieh March 27, 2013_

From: _Your "elder" sister Always, Jo_

Other books by Gregory E. Lang:

*Why a Daughter Needs a Dad*

*Why a Son Needs a Dad*

*Why I Love Grandma*

*Why I Love Grandpa*

*Why a Son Needs a Mom*

*Why a Daughter Needs a Mom*

*Why I Chose You*

*Why I Love You*

*Why I Still Love You*

*Why I Need You*

*Why We Are a Family*

*Why We Are Friends*

*Brothers and Sisters*

*Simple Acts*

*Love Signs*

*Life Maps*

*Thank You, Mom*

*Thank You, Dad*

# Sisters

## · 100 Ways They Bless Our Lives ·

GREGORY E. LANG AND
JANET LANKFORD-MORAN

CUMBERLAND HOUSE

NASHVILLE, TENNESSEE

SISTERS
PUBLISHED BY CUMBERLAND HOUSE PUBLISHING, INC.
431 Harding Industrial Drive
Nashville, TN 37211

ISBN-13: 978-1-58182-688-3
ISBN-10: 1-58182-688-5

Cover design: JulesRulesDesign
Cover photograph: Fotosearch/SassyStock
Text design: Lisa Taylor
Interior photographs: Janet Lankford-Moran and Gregory E. Lang


Printed in Canada
1 2 3 4 5 6 7 8 — 13 12 11 10 09 08

To Jamie—you are cherished. Love you.
—Janet

To Meagan and Linley
—Big G.

# INTRODUCTION

Having entered the world thirteen years after my parents' first child, I am the youngest of three children. Born into a well-seasoned family far beyond the baby stage in life, my parents, who were in their early forties when I was born, happily embraced my unexpected arrival. I was indeed a detour in their plans—as I entered the first grade my brother was enrolling in college, and my sister, Jamie, began high school.

As children Jamie and I did all the carefree things siblings do together. We shared a bedroom, where we would sometimes stay up later than we were supposed to, confiding in each other or just being silly. We played tricks on one another, kept each other's secrets, and shared a special kinship that was a mystery to our parents and older brother.

My family encountered a second, more dramatic, detour when I was eight years old. My mother passed away, and my father suddenly found himself with a teenage daughter and a young child to care for by himself. With the absence of a mother in our home, my father turned to my older sister to help raise me, especially in an area where he had no clue: the mysteries of a young feminine mind.

Rather than feel resentful or put upon, Jamie embraced her new role in my life with the nurturing love and understanding only a sister could naturally give. She helped me navigate the mysteries of choosing a bra, understanding boys, and getting a period. She filled the shoes of a mother in those touchy areas, and she did it with grace.

Yet, in spite of Jamie's best efforts to take care of me, her duel role of sister and surrogate mother was difficult to maintain. As sisters usually do, we had our times of tribulation. When you're in high school, having a little sister tag along all the time can be tiresome. Equally frustrating for me was having an older sister who wielded so much authority over me. If I had a friend or boyfriend she didn't approve of my father knew about it. Somehow we coexisted through these times, though, and learned the importance of conflict resolution.

When I left home to attend college, we came to a truce, which allowed us to remain fond of each other. Jamie had three little ones and was in the throes of motherhood. I watched her develop a new identity as "Mother," and she watched me become an adult. We were close, but our lives were more different than ever.

Many years have passed since we lived together in the comfortable nest of our childhood home, but the special bond that ties us together has not diminished. In fact, it has grown. I was awakened to the sacrifices my parents made for me after the birth of my first child. I also realized I hadn't placed enough value on the role my sister played in my life and development. The birth of my son, Henry, led me to think back to what Jamie went through while standing in for my mother. For the first time, I understood her sacrifices and her loss of patience with me.

My sister has given me a lifelong feeling of continuity. She grounds me in a history that keeps me humble and appreciative and fills me with a sense of belonging. She provides me with companionship I can always count on and enjoy. She makes me laugh. She gives me a kind of love that cannot be found elsewhere.

Now made wiser by my years and life experiences, I more than ever appreciate all the roles sisters play in one another's lives: best friend, trusted advisor, unselfish caregiver, even safe-keeper of our deepest secrets. We women depend on our sisters in different ways at different times throughout our lives, be it during the turmoil of the teen years, in marriage, preparing for the birth of a child, or dealing with the death of a loved one. Having a sister in my life, one who has given me abundant love and support over the years, was central to helping me become the daughter, wife, and mom—indeed, the *woman*—I am today.

In taking the photographs for this book, I wanted to illustrate the variety of sororal relationships and the ways these siblings come together to celebrate and nurture their love. For two young sisters, it might be a tea party or an afternoon of dress up and pretend play. For older sisters, it might be cooking a family meal together, sewing an heirloom quilt, or just reminiscing over coffee. Having experienced my own sister not only as a sibling but as a mother and now a best friend, I wanted, in some small way, to give a voice to the bond felt by all sisters that is both universal and unique.

With this book I also wanted to tell Jamie "thank you" for all she has done for me, to give applause to all the time and effort she invested in making sure I didn't run amok, and to hold her out as a shining example of just what a great gift from God sisters are for one another.

I love you, Jamie. Thanks for everything.

*Janet J. Moran*

# SISTERS

# Sisters

always make time to play together.

■ ■ ■ ■ ■ ■

# Sisters

are God's way of making sure a child is never lonely.

# Sisters

understand each other's idiosyncrasies.

*can't help but get into a little mischief
now and then.*

know when to give each other a little time and space.

# Sisters . . .

plan together for how best to take care of their parents.

offer comfort when one is afraid.

provide guidance for one another so that nobody
in the family feels lost.

# Sisters

can see through each other's facade.

■      ■      ■      ■      ■      ■      ■

# Sisters

understand each other in a way that no one else can.

# Sisters . . .

support each other in all of life's challenges.

are always there for each other,

without exception.

share a love that grows and never fades.

# Sisters

are there to help each other

when time takes its toll.

*are lifelong best friends.*

never get too old to hug one another.

# Sisters

watch over each other with love and affection.

■    ■    ■    ■    ■    ■

# Sisters . . .

stand up for one another in times of doubt.

can say things to one another that no one else can.

know how far to take a joke
without going too far.

challenge one another to help one another grow.

# Sisters

are each other's most loyal fan.

■    ■    ■    ■    ■    ■

# Sisters

look up to and respect one another.

*forgive one another without having to be asked.*

sacrifice for the benefit of each other.

# Sisters

conspire to keep their parents young.

# Sisters

revel in each other's goofiness.

# Sisters

may grow up but never grow apart.

# Sisters

are unable to stay mad at each other for very long.

# Sisters

are the cornerstones in one another's lives—

always there to hold each other up.

*are each other's cherished connection*

*to the past.*

know when to laugh and when to comfort.

encourage one another when the going gets tough.

# Sisters . . .

strive to overcome their differences.

don't just stand by and watch when one
of their own is down and out.

always offer a shoulder to lean on.

do not shy away from each other's tears.

# Sisters

protect each other from harm.

# Sisters

can get on each other's nerves,
but always get over it.

■    ■    ■    ■    ■    ■

# Sisters

are the best present parents can give.

# Sisters

include each other in all the fun stuff.

■ ■ ■ ■ ■ ■

# Sisters . . .

give each other tough love when necessary.

understand one another's pain, but never let
each other wallow in it.

need each other to better understand their parents.

need each other to better understand their homework.

# Sisters

look forward to seeing each other
after times of separation.

■    ■    ■    ■    ■    ■    ■

# Sisters

are there for each other when it seems no one else is.

■　　　■　　　■　　　■　　　■　　　■　　　■

# Sisters

give each other some of the best advice.

■    ■    ■    ■    ■    ■

# Sisters . . .

teach each other how to do things for themselves.

won't let one another make major mistakes.

won't put up with less than should be expected
of each other.

call each other now and then just to say "hello."

# Sisters

can communicate without using words.

# Sisters

understand that in teasing laughter there is love.

# Sisters

protect each other from monsters, bullies,
and broken hearts.

# Sisters

won't let distance keep them apart.

*are sensitive to each other's tender spots.*

let each other bask in the spotlight on birthdays.

help each other to remember the important things
that may have been forgotten.

# Sisters

love to tell those old, embarrassing stories
over and over again!

■     ■     ■     ■     ■     ■     ■

# Sisters

will do their best to keep one another
from getting into trouble.

# Sisters

learn some of life's most valuable lessons from each other.

# Sisters

become trusted keepers of each other's children.

# Sisters

aspire to be like one another.

■     ■     ■     ■     ■     ■

# Sisters

make a family last forever.

■   ■   ■   ■   ■   ■

# Sisters

share what they have for the pleasure of all.

*can have fun doing nothing.*

enjoy a little competition once in a while.

# Sisters

never tire of each other's company.

# Sisters

have a way of knowing what's on each other's mind.

# Sisters

can fill a treasure chest with wonderful memories.

*can be counted on to keep a secret.*

won't let you get away with things
you shouldn't get away with.

have the best pillow fights.

# Sisters

sometimes show their love in unique ways.

# Sisters

know how to keep the party rocking!

■     ■     ■     ■     ■     ■

# Sisters

lend helping hands without expectation of reward.

# Sisters . . .

always watch each other's back.

play hide and seek.

keep each other humble.

help each other with the chores.

# Sisters

stick together like peanut butter and jelly.

# Sisters

make a house a fun place to live.

# Sisters . . .

always take one another's phone calls, no matter

how late it might be.



pass family traditions from generation to generation.



make the best shopping buddies.

# Sisters

never keep score or hold grudges.

# Sisters

do not betray each other.

# Sisters

take turns being the line leader.

# Sisters

can't help but make fun of each other once in a while.

*make each other's life more fun!*

help each other to look their best.

# Sisters . . .

never tire of telling each other, "I love you."

can cheer you up like no one else can!

do things for one another without having to be asked.

# Sisters

seem to show up in each other's life
at just the right time.

■   ■   ■   ■   ■   ■

# Sisters

can put a smile on each other's face
in a split second.

# Sisters

share a bond that cannot be found anywhere else.

# Sisters

do not hesitate to show their affection for each other.

Paste your picture here and
write your thoughts
on the opposite page.

# Sisters

# To Contact the Authors

*write in care of the publisher:*
Cumberland House Publishing
431 Harding Industrial Drive
Nashville, TN 37211

*or e-mail the authors:*
greg.lang@mindspring.com
janet@oijoyphoto.com

*visit the authors' Web sites:*
gregoryelang.com
oijoyphoto.com